Love One Another
How To Grow Spiritually

Denna E. Day

WestBow
PRESS
A DIVISION OF THOMAS NELSON

WestBow Press books may be ordered through booksellers or by contacting:

WestBow Press
A Division of Thomas Nelson
1663 Liberty Drive
Bloomington, IN 47403
www.westbowpress.com
1-(866) 928-1240

Library of Congress Control Number: 2012917257

ISBN: 978-1-4497-6792-1 (sc)
ISBN: 978-1-4497-6793-8 (e)

Printed in the United States of America

WestBow Press rev. date: 09/20/2012

Dedication

———∞∞∞———

This book is dedicated to my Grandfather, the late Joshua McKinley Russ Jr., a man of great faith and epitome of love. He affectionately expressed and demonstrated his love to all his children, grandchildren, and great-grandchildren every opportunity he had.

Acknowledgements

———— ∞∞∞ ————

Special thanks to my husband, Marion Day and sister, Danna Pittman for their assistance with writing this book. Also, my friend Dara Hudson for her contributions in editing. Thank you to my Lord and Savior Jesus Christ.

Table of Contents

June 21, 2012

Foreword
By Danna Suzette Pittman

———⚬⚬⚬———

I am abundantly **BLESSED** and honored to write the foreword for an amazing woman of faith in God. I am the right person to write the foreword because no one else can say they met Evangelist Denna Day in the womb. Yes, we are identical twins! How cool is that? We are twenty minutes apart. The first mention of twins is noted in Genesis 25:26 – *Then the other twin was born with his hand grasping Esau's heel.* I laugh today because I am on her heels in the Spirit. However, our mother's story is that

Evangelist Day pushed me back into the womb, and she was born first.

I am married to a loving husband of twenty-five years with one handsome son. Words cannot express how I feel about Evangelist Day stepping out on faith and taking an unimaginable risk of revealing her personal journey of trials, disappointments, and redemption.

"Love is the greatest gift above prophecy, discernment, speaking in tongues, Hallelujah! Love one another." Notice the awesome beginning to chapter three of Evangelist Day's book. She reminds us that we all have spiritual gifts working in our lives; we are not complete without the gift of LOVE prevailing in each of us. Evangelist Day had to overcome rejection at church by some leaders and members, then again around friends who felt like they could not be themselves. Through it all, she never wavered from her purpose. One of Evangelist Day's favorite quotes from Shakespeare is, "To thine own self, be true."

Moreover, I thank God that she is at this point in time for His glory. Through her faith in God, she has been able to push past mountains in her path of promotion--denials, being silenced in churches, and multiple bouts of depression. Then she overcame those obstacles by, "loving the unlovable", as she so graciously stated in the book.

Colossians 3:16-17 NLT – Let the message about Christ, in all its richness, fill your lives. Teach and counsel each other with all the wisdom He gives. Sing psalms and hymns and spiritual songs to God with thankful hearts. And whatever you do or say, do it as a representative of the Lord Jesus, giving thanks through Him to God the Father.

I am encouraged by my sister's love in God and you will be too. My prayer is that through reading this book, you will be able to overcome your personal journeys of trials and disappointments by loving one another through Christ who loves us. God bless you and your family. Amen.

Danna Suzette Pittman

Introduction

───◈◈◈───

I share personality traits and my family history in the first two chapters. In chapter three I had the privilege of delivering a sermon to a local church and was led to speak on the subjects of love and spiritual growth. Thus is my inspiration to have written this book, and I would like to share it with others. I feel it is a part of my calling as both Evangelist and teacher to share my gifts in order to get more people "on fire" for the Lord. I also take you on a journey of the importance of giving, finding ways to bounce back after you've been knocked down, seeing yourself as God sees you, and not allowing divorce as an option in my house.

CHAPTER 1

I Am An Introvert

---⟨≋⟩---

(Jeremiah 1:5-8 NKJV) "Before I formed you in the womb I knew you; before you were born I sanctified you; I ordained you a prophet to the nations," Then said I: "Ah, Lord God! Behold, I cannot speak, for I am a youth." But the Lord said to me: Do not say, "I am a youth," for you shall go to all to whom I send you, and whatever I command, you shall speak. Do not be afraid of their faces, for I am with you to deliver you, "says the Lord.

The Lord will give us instructions to go forth and in the midst of our obedience, He will set you free from the spirit of I cannot. (Philippians 4:13 NKJV) *I can do all things through Christ who strengthens me.* All He needs is willing and obedient servants to spread the good news and to speak whatever God tells us to speak. Jesus has delivered me from shame, heartbreak, and alcohol abuse. The fire comes to strengthen God's people and to look more like a siliceous rock. (John 15:5 NKJV) *"I am the vine, you are the branches. He who abides in Me, and I in him, bears much fruit; for without Me, you can do nothing."*

I completed a couple of personality type, (self-scored) exercises, and I am truly an Introvert with a triangle shaped behavior. How many people believe that God will give you boldness to accomplish His works? Introverts are people who tend to focus on their inside world while isolated and detached from others. However, God does not want us isolated and distant from other people. He wants us to grow together, just like wheat and tares. When we keep away from people, we gain our own ideas that may be foolish if not submitted under wise counsel. (Proverbs 18:1-2 NKJV) *A man who isolates himself seeks his own desire; He rages against all wise Judgment. A fool has no delight in understanding, but in expressing his own heart.* As one who has a sensing personality trait, I've found that I focus on the present energy around me, able to discern different spirits, "judging by evidence whether those spirits are evil or of God" (Vines Expository Dictionary). As a feeling type, I tend to base most of my decisions primarily on the worth of something and my own personal biases, sometimes to the point of being selfish. My perceptive side, however, allows me to take risks and approach life making quick decisions while keeping my options open.

I can be alone without having to keep busy. Quiet time helps me wind down from a long day or reflect on what needs to be done. I dislike meaningless conversation because there is no interest in them for me. However, I will come together with family to enjoy their company. When I meet someone for the first time, normally I am at a loss for words. You can literally encourage or discourage a person through perception. On the other hand, fellowship with the saints brings growth.

> *(Hebrew 10:24-25 NKJV) And let us consider*
> *one another in order to stir up love and*
> *good works, not forsaking the assembling of*
> *ourselves together, as is the manner of some,*
> *but exhorting one another, and so much*
> *the more as you see the Day approaching.*

True story, my husband deep-fried two turkeys for one of his co-workers. When the woman came to collect the turkeys, she brought her husband and they wanted to meet me. I thought they would stay outside, take the turkeys, then leave. No, they wanted my husband to introduce me. Well, I ran upstairs before they could see me. I told my husband I am not decent, and it would be better to meet them another time. My introversion kicked in and I began to focus on the inner world of ideas and impressions. I thought they would judge me and I was not prepared for them. My husband was disappointed in me, so I told him

I will meet them next time. Unfortunately, next time never came.

If God is not using me on the streets as a soul winner or if I'm in my comfort zone with friends and family members, I would not be a social butterfly attempting to know everyone in the room. Whatever your personality type, whether an introvert or extrovert, love yourself and don't compromise. You will sleep better at night.

CHAPTER 2

Reflections of My Life

⟡

As I take this time to reflect on the passage of my life, I can truly say that I am somewhat pleased with the generation era I am a part of. I was born September 6, 1967, twenty minutes before my identical twin sister was born. The reason it was twenty minutes is because the doctors didn't know my mother was having twins. There were no ultrasounds performed to determine how many babies or the gender. I feel astonished some nights when I think about the journey life has taken me through. The year I was born, Lyndon B. Johnson was the President of the United States. He was appointed following the assassination of John F. Kennedy. Since then I have lived through eight other Presidents.

In the 1960's and 1970's, we lost a few good men, two of whom were great African Americans. Dr. Martin Luther King Jr., was a Civil Rights Activist, who preached non-violence, unity, and equality. It's honorable to have a holiday named after a wise and imperfect man. In contrast to his teachings, Malcolm X was a Black Muslim that taught white hatred. Even if it took violence, then violence it was. Both men were murdered because of their beliefs in justice for all—all need inclusion and equal rights. There were years of oppression endured by the Black community. The African American community had come a long way; however, it still had a long way to go. Heavy drug use started across the country, from marijuana to heroin, and from LSD to PCP.

Then from the 1980's until today, crack rock cocaine and other drugs created such a dependency to cause people to lose everything they had. Some lost their families, cars, houses, and even their lives. HIV and AIDS arose as crucial problems in our society as well. Drugs and diseases, though two different issues, became very deadly. I myself have seen what drugs can do first hand.

My brother suffered from schizophrenia, and was institutionalized several times over approximately thirty years before his death in 2009. He had a lifelong struggle with drugs and alcohol. I miss him very much. When he let me pray for him, T.A. would say, "Denna got some sweet prayers." I'm blessed that I was able to tell him I love him before his death. I forgave him for the pain he caused the family.

(Matthew 11:28-30 NKJV) "Come to Me, all you who labor and are heavy laden, and I will give you rest. Take My yoke upon you and learn from Me, for I am gentle and lowly in heart, and you will find rest for your souls. For my yoke is easy and My burden is light."

(Isaiah 59:1 NKJV) Behold, the Lord's hand is not shortened, that it cannot save; nor His ear heavy, that it cannot hear.

I honestly believe that society along with government saw the struggle in our generation, and it created equal opportunity and the right to compete. Don't quote me, but during the Reagan years, free enterprise was launched and helped many Americans earn a healthy and prosperous living. Also, policies and procedures for sexual harassment were put into the workplace when it hadn't been in the past. Music even exploded with videos attached to it, thanks to MTV and BET.

Growing up I was very athletic because in high school I played basketball, softball, and ran track. I didn't go to the hospital for anything major, only a few minor bumps and bruises. I was normal weight for the longest time. My parents were great providers because we didn't lack for anything. All of our needs were met. I was raised in a house in a small town called Port St. Joe, Florida. We had a fig tree, pear tree, apple tree, banana tree and a pecan tree, and my most favorite of all was the muscadines. I didn't know anything about "the projects" until I graduated and moved to Miami, FL. Moving from a small town to a large city like Miami after graduation was a major transition in my life.

(Matthew 13:8 NKJV) But others fell on good ground and yielded a crop: some a hundredfold, some sixty, some thirty.

We ate healthy during the cohort years because my parents owned a farm, which they live on now. They moved in 1994 about 70 miles east of where I grew up. Every summer we had to pick peas, corn, and okra. Next we had to shell the peas and shuck the corn. I despised those chores because it took away our time from friends, but now I understand and appreciate why we had to plant, pick, pluck, can and preserve our own food. My mother today still talks about how she loves to walk outside and pick what she wants to eat every day. Now in my 40's, I understand that we were taught the sowing and reaping principle as children. The right soil yields the best crops. My parents sold and even gave away some crops because of the abundance.

Biologically my weight began to change and when I became pregnant, I added about fourteen pounds to my small frame body. I nursed my son for one year after his birth. I was told to eat foods that helped produce milk. I think it was vegetables and beef, but whatever the diet was, I gained more pounds than I wanted. I haven't been successful at losing a certain amount of and keeping it off for a long time.

Although I'm at risk of diabetes and high blood pressure because it runs in the family, I thank God I don't have any health problems today. I used to take Alprazolam and high blood pressure medication, but not anymore. I am healed in Jesus' name. All I need to do now is walk briskly at least three days a week, eat healthier, and sleep longer to enjoy a fun-filled life with my family. Then maybe I can live as long as my Grandfather who lived until he was 102 years old.

CHAPTER 3

Love Is the Greatest Gift

⸺∞⸺

Love is the greatest gift above prophecy, discernment, speaking in tongues. Love one another. I have a definition of love. According to *Merriam-Webster's Pocket Dictionary,* love is a strong affection, warm attachment. According to *VINE'S Expository Dictionary of Old and New Testament Words*, phileo represents tender affection. Love does not hurt. You take pleasure in love. (1Corinthians 13 KJV) speaks much on the subject of love. I am beginning there because I feel am being delivered to do so.

A captive audience shows support by clapping and using words of encouragement. "That's all right. Come on. I stand with you." I start out with the words, "Can you love the unlovable? Can you do it?" as joyful praises of "Hallelujah!" ring out. My voice trembles slightly, but I continue onward. "When you go and greet somebody and they turn away, can you love them? Even out on the streets soul winning, minister to everyone, including those who are under demonic influences and bound by addictions. We must love the unlovable." *Though I speak with the tongues of men and of angels and have not charity, I am become as sounding brass or a tinkling cymbal.* "Now that's love," I think to myself. I urge the drummer to hit that cymbal, and as if on cue, "Ting!" and more Hallelujahs vibrate in the small, but cozy church. "You're just making a lot of noise," I profess to the crowd, "I don't feel any warmth. I don't feel any affection." Some of the ladies would shout, "I love you, Sister Denna". "You do? Where is the warmth? You're just making some noise in here. But I want you to love me because I love you."

If I don't love anybody, how will anybody love me? I first have to love myself. Speaking of which, I remember years ago, some of my girlfriends and I would sit around singing, praying, and having fun. We would joke around occasionally with the gift of tongues by saying things that sounded like "come tie my tie" and "send him in a Cadillac" rapidly spurted out. (Laughing out loud) Occasionally, we would have twelve hour prayer, from six p.m. Friday evening until six a.m. Saturday morning. What a joyous time basking in the presence of the Lord!

Though I have the gift of prophecy, and understand mysteries, and knowledge. And though I have faith so I can remove mountains and I have not love, I have nothing. And though I bestow all my goods to feed the poor, and give my body to be burned and have not love, then it profits me nothing. Charity suffers long. Let me say that again; it suffers long. You must have patience to love people. You need patience because there are so many devils that test our longevity and patience, most of whom do not even believe in Jesus. Many religions do believe in God, just not His son, Jesus.

My co-workers worked on me one day. (I am laughing.) My love walk was tested, and I did not tell anyone I was going to preach until 5:30 p.m., fifteen minutes before the end of my shift and an hour or so before actually speaking to the congregation. Many asked, "Why didn't you tell us you were speaking today?" I replied, "Because I didn't want you to know." I might have messed up. I'm suffering long with you. They tried me today, but I was quiet. One friend told me that in such occasions, I should keep my head low and my mouth closed, and that is what I did. One lady would come over and say, "What's wrong with Denna today?" With my mouth silent, my eyes answered, "I'm trying to love you." Hallelujah!

Love is kind, and it's not puffed up. It's not jealous or boastful; it's neither proud nor rude. Love is gentle and it's agape, unselfish love, unconditional love. Whether the saints hug or not when they try to greet one another continue love. *Doth not behave itself unseemly, seeketh not her own, is not easily provoked, thinketh no evil.* When I was fired from one of my jobs, my manager drove an SUV, and I wanted to cut two of her tires because I believed she wronged me. It's only by the grace of God I didn't. *Rejoice not in iniquity, but rejoiceth in the truth.* I like one of Shakespeare's quote, "to thine own self, be true." I have carried this statement for a long time. One particular Pastor preached a message that seemed tailor-made just for me, and I used to think it's not for me. Then I began to say, "yes, it's me, it's me oh Lord. Oh Lord it's me!"

It bares all things, believeth all things, hopeth all things, endureth all things. Charity (love) never fails. But whether there be prophecies they shall fail, and whether there be tongues they shall cease, and whether there be knowledge it shall vanish away. For we know in part, and we prophesy in part. But when that which is perfect is come, then that which is in part shall be done away. When we come in the full understanding, and full knowledge of God, the whole from Genesis to Revelations, we begin to grow and mature in the ways of God! Our dreams and visions become realized, for that which is perfect is going to come. All other stuff is going to be done away with. The eleventh verse *when I was a child, I spake as a child, I understood as a child, I thought as a child, but when I became a man (or woman), I put away childish things* is talking about spiritual immaturity. One is immature if he or she is acting like a child. It's time for us to grow up in God and mature in God. Hallelujah!

Now I am going to give a testimony. I got saved when I was twenty-two years old. Hallelujah! I was running for my life, running for the Lord, learning in church Monday, Wednesday, Thursday, and Friday as part of Leadership Training. Then Sunday, I was in church again. But I didn't mind, hallelujah! So as I began to grow in God and in the knowledge of God. I got puffed up. I once tried to blame my Pastors for hindering my spiritual progress and delaying or stalling my ministry. It was their fault, and they were the reasons I was not where I was supposed to be because they offended me. But when I got to a later ministry, this lovely man and lovely woman said, "You need to forgive." I protested because they hurt me, but they insisted it had to be done.

I remember a time when there were so much going on and I was all up in their faces contradicting them. They would say, "Denna you can't sing today; sit down, Denna." It was not in the literal sense. They silenced me and even disallowed me from participating in any help ministries for a year. That was me then because I thought I was a Prophet. I thought I could prophesy. These are just some reasons why I decided to move to Tampa, Florida. I just got mad and left. Since I was still hurting, I took flight. God has a way of dealing with His people.

I didn't forgive until years later which caused a bitter root to spring up. (Hebrew 12:15 KJV) *Looking diligently lest any man fail of the grace of God; lest any root of bitterness springing up trouble you, and thereby many be defiled.* When things trouble you and you have no peace, it means a problem has never been dealt with. Once I wrote a letter to my ex-pastors and truly forgave, I felt in my natural heart a root literally being pulled out, and it hurt like someone had pinched me. It's just like harvesting potatoes, which grow underground. You can't see the bitterroot growing, but it's present. When you pull the stem, the whole potato and root comes up together, out of the ground. This is the best I can describe of the relief and healing I felt at that moment.

Psychoanalyst, Karen Horney, says neurotic adjustment to other people deals with inner conflict, and we find ourselves moving toward people where we give in, agreeing to everything because we do not want to be hurt anymore. If we become hostile or initiate arguments with another or move against people, we have power and no one can hurt us. So, in essence, when a person withdraws, it means nothing can hurt them, and they become detached. I recommend faith towards God because if you trust Him with your life, He will provide you with His comfort and security. Surrender all to God and he will direct your path.

(Job 13:15 NKJV) Though He slay me, yet will I trust Him. Even so, I will defend my own ways before Him. (Psalm 118:8 NKJV) It is better to trust in the Lord than to put confidence in man.

CHAPTER 4

Give Unto the Lord

———⦿⦿⦿———

(Matthew 6:1-2 KJV) *Take heed that ye do not your alms before men, to be seen of them: otherwise ye have no reward of your Father which is in heaven. Therefore, when thou doest thine alms, do not sound a trumpet before thee, as the hypocrites do in the synagogues and in the streets, that they may have glory of men. Verily I say unto you: They have their reward. When you give to someone in need don't be a hypocrite, blowing a trumpet for everyone to see. If you do, then you have your reward.* That's when you have your praise. When you say boastful things, bragging about what you have done for another, that simple and meager praise is your reward, and God gets no glory from that. In essence, most people do not care what you do for others anyway. Give unto the Lord in secret and He will bless you openly. The heart has to be right in all we do.

Lend to people, expecting a return because every seed sown must produce a harvest. This means we who are spiritual definitely have to release the people that hurt us. If we hold on, the pain stops mobility in ministering to others in need. In 2010 a single mother asked me to loan her some money. She was unemployed at the time, and we agreed that she could pay me when she finds a job. Well, since that time, she moved out of her home and did not inform me. I went to visit her one day and a whole different family was living there.

Next, she was seen at an NFL event and she was asked to call me. She had the nerve to suggest I call her, knowing her cellular number was different and I didn't have the new number. So, I began to send her messages over Facebook because she would not confirm my friendship. The last message I sent was, "I release you from the debt you owe me. God has blessed me!" God has given me so much more than what she has stolen.

(2 Cor. 9:6-8 NKJV) *But this I say: He who sows sparingly will also reap sparingly, and he who sows bountifully will also reap bountifully. So let each one give as he purposes in his heart, not grudgingly or of necessity; for God loves a cheerful giver. And God is able to make all grace abound toward you, that you, always having all sufficiency in all things, may have an abundance for every good work.* The cheerful giver has a great attitude and measures the amount when it comes to giving. Giving is not just on Sundays, but every day of the week. A giver will give to someone in need. Give people your best and not garbage because our heavenly Father gives His best. If you do not give, expect lack in your life. Limits in your giving means limits in the anointing. I need the anointing in ministry, soul winning, and finances.

(Luke 16:10-13) He who is faithful in what is least is faithful also in much: and he who is unjust in what is least is unjust also in much. "Therefore, if you have not been faithful in

the unrighteous mammon, who will commit
to your trust the true riches? "And if you have
not been faithful in what is another man's,
who will give you what is your own? "No
servant can serve two masters; for either he
will hate the one and love the other, or else
he will be loyal to the one and despise the
other. You cannot serve God and mammon.

Be faithful where the Lord has you and behold what He does in your life. Give ten percent of what you want to earn on a monthly basis and watch how God open doors you would never imagine. I did that and my income increased by ten thousand dollars the same year and would go on to increase thirteen thousand more dollars over a three year period. We were tithers to the local church and we gave to friends, family, and people in need. He made us a blessing to bless others. It is a great joy when I can help someone in need. The expression on a thankful and grateful face is more satisfying than me going out to buy something nice for myself.

While worshiping in a Sunday night service, a Mexican man that sat on the row in front of me turned around and gave me $100. He said, "It's from the Lord." I walked in the isle and started praising God. When I went back to my seat, a Caucasian woman walks up to me saying, "The Lord told me to write you a check for $500. " My mind was blown away. I handed my driver license and a pen over to the woman. She told me she was from Texas. I shared with her my husband was the only one working and I am not receiving any government assistance. The Lord told me to walk by faith. I left a high-paying, five figure a year job months ago without any government food stamps or unemployment checks.

Jehovah Jireh is my provider. I was amazed at all He had done in that service. That is one thing Jesus has done to prove His love towards me. I didn't know those people. But God knew them and I pray He continues to bless and multiply their seed over and over again.

I was in a take-out pizza place to buy a pizza and wings for lunch. I had a $100 bill and I thought to myself, I'll just pay cash to change the bill. Unction from the Holy Spirit caused me to pay by debt card. A lady pushing a baby carriage and a son about five years old was next to me. As I turned to open the door, the mother told her son to open the door for me. My heart went out to them. I said, "Do you know God has a wonderful plan for your life?" She said, "Yes." We engaged in a conversation, which directed me to bless that single mother with two kids with the $100. The little boy leaped saying, "Mom look! It's a hundred dollars!" As I opened the door and sat in my car, immediately a scripture leaped out of my heart.

(Galatian 6:9 KJV) And let us not be weary in well doing: for in due season we shall will reap, if you faint not.

I helped a woman in my church with her car repair. The next day she said, "Denna let me give you another hug for obeying God." I paid a bill and bought food for my first ladies luncheon. Four out of seven of those ladies gave their hearts to the Lord because three of them were already saved.

(Galatians 6:10 KJV) As we have therefore opportunity, let us do good

*unto all men, especially unto them
who are of the household of faith.*

Chapter 5

Repercussions of Backsliding

~~~~~~

Love never gives up and never loses faith and is always hopeful. I was out there, but I was hopeful. I had some hope in me. My prayer was, "Lord, send me some help. Help me Jesus! I can't do it without you! Lord, help me! I can't do it without you! Help me Jesus!"

I was having a good time, going out to clubs and parties in my middle thirties. I love to dance, and one of my sisters said to me, "Why you all in the club? You act like you missed something! You aren't missing anything." I believe she was saying get back in the church. What are you doing out here woman of God? Everybody knew who I was except me. I'm still talking about love. (See, if she didn't care, she would not have those feelings of love.)

For my sermon, I asked my husband to help me out for a moment because I believe in demonstration. I asked the Pastor if he minded. I pulled out a pair of handcuffs, and the people began to laugh. I said, "Don't go there. I'm talking about something pure, and just." God has a way to get your attention though. While going to clubs and parties, I was privately praying help me. What happened next would change my life forever. The Lord allowed blue and red lights to get my attention because I was overriding the Holy Ghost. Glory to God! I was attending church and I was fasting that day, but I wanted to please my friend and I went to a birthday party at a mall. I didn't like going to this particular mall because I was still trying to learn the city, so I knew I would get lost on the way home. The police officer said, "You're speeding?" I replied, "I'm lost." Then he said, "I smell something!" I said, "What do you smell?" "Get out of the car!"

I said, "Oh my God!" "You could have hit my wife and killed her." I shut up. I didn't want to kill anybody. I had to go through a sobriety test. That was one of the most humiliating experiences I've had to endure.

My hands were cuffed in the back and once we arrived at booking, my hands were cuffed in the front. You see, when you are in handcuffs you're in bondage, you are restrained. I was in bondage. That's the picture I tried to instill in the congregation. Marion still being handcuffed, his hands on the back of him, I told him to lift his hands. He said, "I can't!" I said, "Lift up holy hands, Marion?" He replied, "Can't do it!" I said, "Marion, lift up holy hands without wrath or doubt." Yet again, he replied, "Can't do it!" I turned to the audience and said, "You all are playing about being in handcuffs, but I have been handcuffed." You see, I couldn't lift up my hands in handcuffs. I couldn't praise my God. A deputy asked had I been drinking, I told him I hadn't, while vomiting all night. Then they sent a trustee who wanted to know what I had to drink, but still I said nothing. Not being given access to the restroom, I heaved right in front of the door. You cannot praise God like that, hallelujah! Take them handcuffs off me, and save me! Take them off of Marion. The point is you can't praise God like that. I got free, people! I beseeched them to lift up their hands without wrath or doubt; no one was in handcuffs in there. I saw no bounds or restraints. "Lift your hands!" I asked the church congregation, because they were free.

Now let me back up. Six months prior, I was a juror for the same thing, judging somebody for DUI. At that point in my life, I was studying Behavioral Psychology at a local university, so my ego had me believing that I knew behavior. I believed he was drunk because he worked at a bar, and he was swerving in the car early in the morning. There was not enough evidence to prove he was guilty of driving while intoxicated, so what could they prove? During the trial, the Holy Ghost spoke to me and said "INNOCENT." I voted guilty. Six months later, the police stopped me.

When you have a calling on your life, God has a way to command your attention. He will chastise you to let you get it right. My license was taken and 2005 was the worst year of my life. I went to jail in a holding room. It was open with a lot of people. I did not have a cell and I did not want to put on that orange jump suit. I stayed there about eight hours, before my husband bonded me out.

My family constantly advised me to sit down, put the cup down, and make it right. That is love. That is showing me affection by telling me the truth. We all have to be honest with ourselves. I took a long look at myself. That same year I was fired from my job for no reason. They built a case against me because they thought I was going to miss too many days behind the arrest. Moreover, the DUI arrest was reduced to Reckless Driving. I worked community service hours, and one of the jobs was to pick up trash on the side of a highway, miles and miles long. I worked at a thrift shop for a local mission. Poor people would come in to buy socks and underwear with nickels and dimes (crying) and I had one hundred dollars in my pocket. I thought I was going to lose my mind that year. But Jesus brought me out.

(Galatians 5:1) Stand fast therefore
in the liberty wherewith Christ hath
made us free, and be not entangled
again with the yoke of bondage.

Don't be held in a snare. When you are caught up in legal issues and mixed up in trouble, you chance being confused, mentally unclear, and uncertain. Those things really disturbed my composure. I was saved, filled with the Holy Ghost for twelve years, walking in the streets running down devils, telling them, "Thus says the Lord." Telling people they need to be saved. However, because of my hurts, (Hallelujah!) and because of my unbelief in my leaders, I left my place. (Hallelujah!) I should have been preaching! I was disobedient. Stay with me. I'm talking about love now.

Chapter 6

Become God's Diamond

(St. John 13:34-35 NKJV) *"A new commandment I give unto you, that you love one another; as I have loved you, that you also love one another. By this shall all men know that you are my disciples, if you have love one to another."* God gives a command, an order, I give to you that you also love one another as I have loved you. If we love one another, we will be disciples. We will become evangelized; we will walk in our callings. We will walk in authority if we love one another.

The Bible states in (Colossians 3:14-15 NKJV) *But above all these things put on love, which is the bond of perfection. And let the peace of God rule in your hearts, to which also ye are called in one body; and be thankful.* Rule means to be an umpire. Let the peace of God rule your hurts; let it act as an umpire (a man in the audience said, "That is good sister"). Not the world peace, but the peace of God. The Lord spoke to me and said, "Saying I am sorry will stop a lot of delay." People of God we must forgive our leaders immediately for any attacks without concealing vexation. Uproot bitterness against people. We need a solid foundation of repentance, humbleness, and love, because favor, grace and prayer will show us the hand of God. Promotions will come. Character is shaped and redefined. I'm not in handcuffs anymore. I'm not depressed anymore. I'm not unstable nor being tossed to and fro. I am not ashamed. Hallelujah! I am standing firm where God planted, rooted, and grounded me in His kingdom. Hallelujah! I charge you today to love your neighbors as you love yourselves. Love is the greatest gift. I don't care if you can prophesy and pray. I'm talking about me, too. If I can hear and see what's going on in the spirit with a person and don't love them. Something is wrong. Hallelujah! Hallelujah!

(St. John 21:15-17 NKJV) *So when they had eaten breakfast, Jesus said to Simon Peter, "Simon, son of Jonah," do you love Me more than these? He said to Him, "Yes, Lord; You know that I love You." He said to him, "Feed my lambs." He said to him again a second time, "Simon, son of Jonah," do you love Me?" He said to Him, "Yes, Lord; You know that I love you." He said to him, "Tend My sheep." He said to him the third time, "Simon, son of Jonah, "do you love me?" Peter was grieved because He said to him the third time, "Do you love Me?" And he said to Him, Lord You know all things; You know that I love you." Jesus said to him, "Feed My Sheep."* I have made my mind up. I am going to feed the sheep. Feed the sheep means to do the work of an Evangelist, and it is most effective with the gift of love.

There is a scale from one to ten that rates the hardness of a mineral. One is the least hard and ten is the hardest. A diamond is the hardest and most valuable mineral in the earth. Diamonds can stand any pressure or heat without being destroyed. However, they can shatter into small pieces with a sharp blow. When life throws a curve ball of life, don't give in because you're still a diamond. Diamonds are so hard that no other substance can scratch it. I am thankful to be a Diamond in the Kingdom of God.

The past year, I traveled across the country with an organization and met six and seven figure income earners, both men and women. They have reached Diamond status within the company. One day during my personal Bible study I began to read Isaiah. According to *Webster's New World Dictionary and Thesaurus,* the word "flint" means a very hard, siliceous rock, usually gray, that produces sparks when struck against steel. Siliceous is a mineral that starts at a number seven on the Mohs' scale of hardness. (Isaiah 50:7 NKJV) *For the Lord God will help me; therefore I will not be disgraced; therefore I have set my Face like a flint, and I know that I will not be ashamed.*

(Isaiah 51:1KJV) *Hearken (Listen) to me, ye that follow after righteousness, ye that seek the Lord: Look unto the rock whence ye are hewn, and to the hole of the pit whence ye are digged.* I realized I'm already a diamond in God's eyes cut from the rock of Jesus Christ. Glory hallelujah!

(Proverbs 10:22, KJV) *The blessings of the Lord, it maketh rich, and he addeth no sorrow with it.* Exercise your faith and stop trying to make things happen on your own. God gives us joy and increases us without stress and strain.

CHAPTER 7

Results of Divorce

∞∞∞

(I Peter 3:1-2) Wives, likewise, be submissive to your own husbands, that even if some do not obey the word, they, without a word, may be won by the conduct of their wives, when they observe your chaste conduct accompanied by fear.

(I Peter 3:4) Husbands, likewise, dwell with them with understanding, giving honor to the wife, as to the weaker vessel, and as being heirs together of the grace of life, that your prayers may not be hindered.

I have been married 20 years to the same man. My parents have been married for 60 years. What a blessing it is! However, becoming one flesh did not come without a price to pay. After being married for five years, we decided to have a baby. The pregnancy was not what I expected because after five months we had a fight and were separated for six months. Let me begin with, we both were saved filled with the Holy Spirit and attending church regularly. Then one day we auditioned to be an extra in the movie, "The Truman Show", and I was hired, he wasn't. My husband was also transitioning out of the Air Force, and I quit a job that I had worked for twelve years because my emotions were uncontrollable and the movie production needed flexible people to work days and nights. The particular company I was employed at, well no one could take off for anything during certain months.

One day when I came home to tell him I quit my job, he grabbed me and started choking me, telling me, "I hate you". Something deeper happened internally with him, which I didn't know at the time. I didn't find out until months later that he was upset about something totally different. When I first became pregnant, my husband was so happy it was our first baby, and I had to say, "It's not yours". When I said those words, he didn't react, and I thought he knew I was kidding. My son looks just like his father and there was no infidelity. However, his anger didn't manifest until I quit my job.

The first thought was divorce. I went to file for divorce, and the last line of the last page asked a question. Is there any chance of reconciliation? I never turned the paperwork in because he said to me on the phone that he hoped we would be able to reconcile, and after he said that we didn't speak for months. So I called him and said, "If you aren't here when I have this baby, don't come back." He came when I was admitted in the hospital, and we've been together since. The healing process hasn't been easy for us. Even today, the enemy tries to come in and destroy, but God lifts up a standard against him. We sought a marriage counselor back then and one thing the counselor said, that I will always remember is, "Stop saying the word divorce."

James 3:8-10 NKJV But no man can tame the tongue. It is an unruly evil, full of deadly poison. With it we bless our God and Father, and with it we curse men, who have been made in the similitude of God. Out of the same mouth proceed blessing and cursing. My brethren, these things ought not to be so.

For me, divorce became more difficult to comprehend because Jesus taught that if a man wants a divorce to fornicate, he leaves his wife open to commit adultery. (Matthew 5:32 KJV) *But I say unto you, That whosoever shall put away his wife, saving for the cause of fornication, causeth her to commit adultery: and whosoever shall marry her that is divorced committeth adultery.* When I studied Behavioral Psychology I began to research how divorce or separation affects children. But redemption comes through (I Corinthians 6:11). *And such were some of you. But you were washed, but you were sanctified, but you were justified in the name of the Lord Jesus and by the Spirit of God.* Each time I didn't feel the love I desired from my husband, I had divorce in my heart. Then a still, small voice would remind me of the scripture. (Mark 10:9 KJV) *What therefore God hath joined together, let not man put asunder.* My husband would even ask me why was I still with him, and I would tell him it was by the grace of God. It was favor that neither he nor I deserve. I need to say, though, that Marion is a wonderful provider and father to our son.

When I studied Behavioral Psychology I began to research how divorce or separation affects children. In my studies, researchers found that children's grades would drop two or three letter grades. Some are affected emotionally, which causes behavioral, physical or psychological problems. Divorce takes a toll on diverse groups of people, regardless of age, race, or sex. It is a common misconception that divorce is for the "good" of the children. Divorce seemingly makes for a calmer environment in the end, but it causes a lot of stress on the adult and child in the beginning.

Although some studies have shown that divorce has no outward or outright effect on children, it may have some inward or long-term effect. Some children develop regressive behavior, become somatic or develop physical ailments such as headaches and nausea. Other children become anxious and display sorrow or sadness. Children often believe they are the ones that caused the divorce and often become blaming and opposing towards one or both parents, or themselves.

The emotional differences of the effects of divorce are inherent between males and females. Though it is hard to conclude what types of effects divorce has because many studies have conflicting information. Some say males become more aggressive, but others show males as not being affected at all. Studies on females show they become depressed and distracted. But most studies agree that the problems seen in children are due to the parents' psychological problems.

Three out of four studies, which I personally conducted, proves divorce has caused headaches and nausea in kids. For example, Jess has a daughter from her first husband and her name is Rachael. The child loves both her parents; however, when the divorce became final, Rachael, about seven at the time, went with her mother.

Jess married a second time to a different man after waiting four or five years, and it destroyed her daughter. Rachael is twelve today and has headaches almost every morning, and now she is scheduled to visit a psychiatrist to determine if it is emotional or physical.

My second participant has two daughters that became part of a nasty divorce. The two daughters decided to go live with their father because their mother was often traveling while enlisted in the Army. The mother is the one that has to pay the child support. Her children, ages 13 and 15, had maintained grades of A's and B's. The only thing wrong is that they wanted to be emancipated because they do not want to be with either parent. The kids became rebellious and stubborn.

Participant number three was a couple that went through a divorce with a nine-year-old son who ended up living with neither parent. He said they argued too much, and he did not want to be around them. He moved with his aunt. Findings show his grades did not drop, and he remained well-mannered.

The fourth participant is Brad. He married a woman that had two kids, ages 13 and 15, with whom he had to use social mobility. After the kids had been verbally abused, Brad had to take his time and show genuine concern for the children, which built up their heir self-esteem and peer mobility. These kids went to college and had families of their own. They joined into activities at school and became more sociable. All because Brad sat down and went over homework and took his time with them. This made a huge difference in the way they perceived their stepdad, and probably other male role models.

(Matthew 19:13-15 NKJV) Then little children were brought to Him that He might put His hands on them and pray, but the disciples rebuked them. But Jesus said, "Let the little children come to Me, and do not forbid them; for of such is the kingdom of heaven." And He laid His hands on them, and he departed from there.

Problems in and around the divorce have a direct impact on children, especially when it is not expected. Unexpected divorce may slow down the amount of time for children to enjoy their childhood. Many divorces tend to affect children's relationships because they often times move out of their familiar settings after parents are divorced. It is hard for children to adapt to a new environment, and after divorce, and it is even more difficult to accept change.

Compared to older children when divorce occurs, younger children become victims; they grow up and do not remember what it was like to have their parents living together. Since divorce is more common among younger couples within the first few years of marriage, they are happier with their parents apart because that is all they have ever known.

There are some things that may prevent the negative types of behavior and experiences the children encounter, one of which is if parents are open and honest with their children. Results show that timing of parental divorce is critical to examine and highlight the importance of assessing the developmental trajectories, including periods both before the divorce and years after the divorce, of children experiencing this major life event. Parents should also spend more quality time with them. Parents should not show anger towards one another when the child is around. It is also not good to make a child feel as though he or she has to choose one parent over the other. Children torn between two parents risk damage to their sense of self-esteem, and there is the potential to cause permanent emotional damage.

I advise all single people to wait on the Lord and He will send you the best, His best. (2Corinthians 6:14NKJV) *Do not be unequally yoked together with unbelievers. For what fellowship has righteousness with lawlessness? And what communion has light with darkness?* He will strengthen you in the darkest hour when no one else is around. I advise married couples to love one another and grow together as one. We must manage our homes and rebuke the devil who wants to destroy our families.

Either we are going to trust God all the way or not. We can't have summer every day; there must be winter seasons in our lives. Today we worship in an International Ministry where the love of God flows to every creation. Be blessed in Jesus' name. If you have not received Jesus as your personal Savior, I preach to you the word of faith.

(Romans 10:9-10 NKJV) That if you confess with your mouth the Lord Jesus and believe in your heart that God has raised Him from the dead, you will be saved. For with the heart one believes unto righteousness, and with the mouth confession is made unto salvation.

Say Jesus, come into my heart. I believe God raised you from the dead. Fill me with the Holy Spirit. Forgive me of your sins. Lord, thank you for saving me. I am saved and on my way to heaven. If you confessed this short prayer, find a local church and plug in, to serve and win the lost. When you are a part of the body of Christ and have faith with works, you will grow spiritually.

Endnotes

⚬⚬⚬

1. Amato, P.R., & Keith, B. (1991). Parental divorce and the well-being of children: A meta-analysis. *Psychological Bulletin*, 110, 26-46.

2. Bates, J.E., Castellino, D.R., Dodge, K.A., Lansford, J.E., Malone, P.S., & Pettit, G.S. (2006). Trajectories of internalizing, externalizing, and grades for children who have and have not experienced their parents' divorce or separation. *Journal of Family Psychology*, 20, 2,292-301.

Author Biography

She gave her life to Christ October 25, 1989 and was baptized by water and the Holy Spirit. While she served in ministry of helps in dance, choir, audio tape, intercessory prayer and leader of a Soul Winning team, she began to experience competition and sabotage. She has a Theology Degree from Day Spring Theological Seminary located in Panama City, FL. She studied Behavioral Psychology with Argosy University in Tampa, FL. She also completed an Associate of Science degree in Business Administration and Management from Gulf Coast Community College.

February 2008, she had the opportunity to partake in sharing a sermon at a local ministry and she believes in sharing love with the world. She is an anointed Evangelist, on fire, proclaiming the word of the Lord to all those who believe that God has plan for their lives. She is a minister of the Lord. She loves to study the word of God, win souls for the Lord, and has a continuous prayer life. The last ten years she has recruited for Colleges and Universities in the Admissions Department and worked in Financial Aid Departments. She is positive that this will be the first of many books to come.

Denna Eyvette Russ was born a twin September 6, 1967 in Port St. Joe, FL. to Mr. and Mrs. Thadus and Lola Russ. She was born twenty minutes before her because the doctors did not know there were two. In 1967, the sonogram had not been invented. She also has three other sisters and two brothers living, along with three deceased brothers. She will celebrate twenty years of marriage September 12, 2012 to Marion Edward Day and they have one son whose name is Daniel Stephen Day. We currently reside in Tampa, FL.